DETERMINED DREAMER

THE STORY OF MARIE CURIE

Written by
Deborah Hopkinson

Illustrated by
Jen Hill

BALZER + BRAY
An Imprint of HarperCollinsPublishers

Marie Skłodowska dreamed of being a scientist.
But for a Polish girl born in 1867
that was a nearly impossible goal.
Marie lived in a time and place
in which few women could go to college,
let alone become scientists and run laboratories of their own.

Yet, from the time she was little, Marie was unstoppable.
She was only four when she snatched a book
from her sister Bronya and began to read aloud.

Everyone stared in astonishment.
When had the baby of the family learned her letters?
"I didn't do it on purpose," Marie cried,
worried that she'd done something wrong.
"It's only because it was so easy!"

Marie was lucky—learning *did* come easily to her.
But her childhood was filled with sorrow too,
when her mama and sister Zofia fell ill and died.
Though she was heartbroken,
Marie kept working hard.

And when she was only fifteen,
Marie graduated from high school at the top of her class.

Marie wanted to follow in her father's footsteps
and study science in college.
But Warsaw University didn't accept women,
so Marie and Bronya, who wanted to be a
doctor, had to move to France to attend
the University of Paris, or the Sorbonne.

Bronya went first, while Marie stayed
behind in Poland to earn money to help support her.
Marie finally set off when she was nearly twenty-four.

As a college student in Paris,
Marie lived six floors up in a tiny room
with just a small coal stove for heat
(and not much money to buy coal).
Brrrr!

On winter nights, she piled up all her clothes on the bed.
Sometimes, in the mornings,
the water in her washbasin had turned to ice.

Most of Marie's classmates were well-educated
young Frenchmen. (Girls were outnumbered almost
a hundred to one.)
Since high school, Marie had been trying to study
on her own, but the other students were more
advanced in math and science.
Marie dived in, determined to catch up.
(She had to learn French too!)
After class, she rushed to the laboratory.

In the evenings, she could be found in the library.
(At least it was heated!)

Then she climbed the stairs to her attic to study more.
Sometimes her only meal was a cup of hot chocolate
with a piece of bread or an egg and fruit.

Despite these hardships, Marie loved her new life.
"All that I saw and learned . . . delighted me," she said.
"It was like a new world opened to me, the world of science."

Marie soon found another love too:
A physicist named Pierre Curie
became her devoted husband

and, later, a loving father to their
daughters, Irène and Ève.

Pierre was also a true research partner
who supported Marie's work and her goal
to become the first woman in France to
earn a doctorate—the highest degree—in
physics.

To do this, Marie needed to choose a research project. She'd been fascinated to hear that a scientist named Wilhelm Röntgen had found mysterious energy waves—called X-rays—which could be used to show bones inside a body.

Soon after, researcher Henri Becquerel discovered a different kind of ray emitted by an element called uranium.

But not much was known about these new rays, so Marie decided to explore more.
She set up a simple, makeshift laboratory at the college where Pierre taught.
She wanted to answer questions such as:
Could radiation be measured?
Were there other substances, besides uranium, that gave off these mysterious rays?

Using a delicate instrument Pierre designed,
Marie learned to precisely measure
the energy given off by uranium.
(Energy means the capacity for doing work. Energy can
exist in many forms, such as wind, waves, or light.)

Then, as Marie was testing a black
ore called pitchblende,
she noticed something puzzling.
Even after the uranium was removed,
strong rays were still being emitted
from the ore.
What could it mean?

Marie could think of only one explanation.
The ore must contain other, unknown
elements with the same capacity as uranium to
produce rays of energy.
Marie decided to call this property *radioactivity*.

And as she continued to test pitchblende,
Marie discovered not one but two new elements
with strong radioactivity.
She named one *polonium*, for her native Poland,
and called the other *radium*, the Latin word for ray.

To show that these truly were new elements, Marie had to separate, or *isolate*, them from pitchblende.

Both are found only in tiny traces. And since isolating polonium seemed nearly impossible, Marie focused on radium.

To isolate radium, Marie had to process several tons of ore dust,
which arrived in sacks speckled with pine needles.
"It was like creating something out of nothing," she said.
Marie's lab was now an abandoned shed,
frigid in winter and sweltering in summer.
"Sometimes I had to spend a whole day mixing a boiling mass
with a heavy iron rod nearly as large as myself," she later wrote.

It took four long years to boil down tons of pitchblende
and crystallize the residue to extract and isolate the radium.
At night, Marie's tiny dishes of radioactive radium salts
made the shed glow with luminous light.

Thanks to her perseverance, Marie was able to extract
about one-tenth of a gram of pure radium
(about the weight of one Cheerio or a small coffee bean).
She had done it at last: in 1902, Marie Curie
became the first person to isolate
the element radium.

Marie's research also brought her to conclude
that radioactivity comes from inside the atom itself.
Marie's insight helped to change the way scientists
thought about the structure of atoms.
It also paved the way for modern physics.

For their work in the new field of radioactivity,
Marie and Pierre, along with Henri Becquerel,
were awarded the Nobel Prize in Physics in 1903.

At first, Marie's name was left off the nomination:
some men couldn't accept that her role had been absolutely critical.
In the end, thanks to Pierre and other fair-minded scientists,
Marie became the first woman to receive a Nobel Prize.

In 1906, Marie faced more heartache
when her beloved Pierre was killed in a traffic accident.
Somehow she found the courage to keep on,
raising her girls and continuing her research.

Eventually Marie's genius was honored
by many who once doubted her.
In fact, Marie became the first person
to receive two Nobel Prizes! Along with the 1903 Nobel Prize
in Physics, in 1911 she was awarded the Nobel Prize in
Chemistry for her discovery of polonium and radium.

When World War I broke out,
Marie knew X-rays could help doctors
to better see and treat a soldier's internal injuries.

But the French army only had one mobile X-ray unit:
not nearly enough for battlefield hospitals.
So the unstoppable Marie sprang into action.

She took a course to learn how to operate an X-ray machine,
secured donations of vehicles and equipment,
and trained young women volunteers to drive and operate
mobile X-ray units called "Petite Curies."

Marie's daughter Irène helped too.
She spent her eighteenth birthday near a battlefield,
taking an X-ray of a soldier's wounded hand
so a doctor could remove four shell fragments.

When the war was over,
Marie continued to study radioactivity.
She became head of the Radium Institute
(now the Curie Institute),
where researchers continue to make discoveries
that build on Marie's work and
her desire to use science to benefit the world.

Today we know radiation has harmful effects
on human cells, causing cancer and other diseases.
And as she grew older, Marie herself suffered from a
blood disease probably caused by exposure to radiation.
She died in 1934, when she was sixty-six.

Marie was a dreamer
who has inspired young people
from all over the world
to become scientists and doctors.

But remember, she began,
just like you,

MARIA
SKŁODOWSKA-CURIE

as a child who wanted to learn.

AUTHOR'S NOTE

Marie Curie led a remarkable life. It's no wonder that more than 150 years after her birth, she remains one of the most admired scientists who ever lived.

As a scientist, Marie broke new ground. It is sometimes hard today to imagine the obstacles she faced. Her lists of accomplishments include becoming the first woman to receive a doctorate of science in France, the first woman to win the Nobel Prize, and the first person to win two Nobel Prizes. She was also the first Nobel Prize winner whose child also became a Nobel Laureate, a distinction Marie shared with her husband, fellow Nobel Prize winner Pierre Curie. After Pierre's death, Marie took on an international role as head of the Radium Institute. Now known as the Curie Institute, the organization continues the Curies' legacy of research dedicated to improving human lives.

Marie forged new roads in other ways, which may seem unremarkable today but were unusual in the nineteenth century. In her marriage to Pierre, she found a partner and a husband who supported her dreams. As a young mother, and later as a single mother to her two daughters, she found ways to balance parenting and her career. Though she is often idealized, Marie Curie was also a real person—a complex woman with strengths and weaknesses. Yet perhaps one of the strongest legacies she leaves us is a reminder of the pure joy of dedication—of giving oneself to fulfilling work to make the world a better place.

Marie wrote a short biography of Pierre after his death. Though she attributes these words to him, it seems clear they both lived by them: "'Whatever happens, even if one should become like a body without a soul, still one must always work.'"

THE LIFE OF MARIE CURIE TIMELINE

1867 Marie is born on November 7 in Warsaw, Poland, as Maria Skłodowska (nicknamed Manya). She is the youngest of five children.

1878 Marie's mother dies of tuberculosis; Marie's eldest sister died in 1876.

1883 Marie graduates best in her class from high school and is awarded a gold medal.

1886 Since women cannot attend Warsaw University, Marie helps to earn money so that her sister Bronya can study in Paris to become a doctor. Marie becomes a governess in the rural town of Szczuki, Poland, spending her free time studying so that someday she can go to college.

1891 Marie enters the University of Paris.

1893 Marie receives her *licence ès sciences physiques*, the French equivalent of a master's degree in physics.

1894 Marie receives her *licence ès mathématiques*, the equivalent of a master's degree in mathematics, and meets Pierre Curie, a French scientist born in 1859.

1895 Marie and Pierre marry on July 26 and spend their honeymoon on a bicycling tour.

1897 Marie and Pierre's first daughter, Irène, is born on September 12. Marie begins her investigation of "Becquerel rays" as her doctoral thesis; Pierre soon joins in her work.

1898 The Curies announce the discovery of two new elements: polonium, in July, and radium, in December; Marie begins her arduous four-year effort to isolate (separate) radium from the ore pitchblende and give it a weight on the periodic table of elements.

1903 Marie receives her doctorate in physics, becoming the first woman in France to receive a doctorate; Marie, Pierre, and Henri Becquerel share the Nobel Prize in Physics for their collective work on radioactivity.

Marie's hypothesis that radioactivity is an atomic property, built into the structure of atoms, would prove to be revolutionary.

1904 Marie gives birth to her second daughter, Ève, on December 6.

1906 Pierre is killed when a horse-drawn wagon runs him over in a busy Paris street on April 19; the University of Paris selects Marie to succeed her husband as professor of physics, and she becomes the university's first female professor.

1909 The University of Paris and the Pasteur Foundation help build the Radium Institute, with Marie heading a radioactivity laboratory. Today, this Paris organization is known as the Curie Institute and includes a scientific research center and hospital.

1911 France's Academy of Sciences refuses to grant Marie membership because she is a woman. She receives the Nobel Prize in Chemistry for the discovery of radium and polonium, becoming the first person to win two Nobel Prizes.

Marie Curie remains the only woman to have won two Nobel Prizes. Linus Pauling is the only person to have won two unshared Nobel Prizes.

1914 World War I begins; Marie and her daughter Irène volunteer and set up mobile X-ray units to help treat wounded soldiers.

1921 Marie makes her first visit to the United States to raise money for the Radium Institute, helping it grow into a world-renowned center for the study of radioactivity.

1934 Irène and her husband, Frédéric Joliot, discover artificial radioactivity, for which they receive the Nobel Prize in Chemistry in 1935.

After suffering from health problems for a number of years, Marie Curie dies on July 4 of a blood disorder probably caused from her longtime exposure to radiation.

SOURCE NOTES

"I didn't do it on purpose . . .": Curie, Ève. *Madame Curie: A Biography*, 9.
"All that I saw and learned . . .": Curie, Marie. *Pierre Curie*, 85.
"'Whatever happens, even if one . . .'": ibid., 43.
"It was like creating . . .": ibid., 91.
"Sometimes I had to spend . . .": ibid., 92.

BIBLIOGRAPHY

Brian, Denis. *The Curies: A Biography of the Most Controversial Family in Science*. Hoboken, NJ: John Wiley & Sons, Inc., 2005.

Curie, Eve. *Madame Curie: A Biography*. Translated by Vincent Sheean. New York: Da Capo Press, 2001. An unabridged republication of the 1937 Doubleday & Co. edition.

Curie, Marie. *Pierre Curie, with Autobiographical Notes by Marie Curie*. Translated by Charlotte and Vernon Kellogg. Mineola, NY: Dover Publications, Inc., 2012. An unabridged republication of the 1923 Macmillan Company edition.

Emling, Shelley. *Marie Curie and Her Daughters*: *The Private Lives of Science's First Family*. New York: Palgrave Macmillan, 2012.

Goldsmith, Barbara. *Obsessive Genius: The Inner World of Marie Curie*. New York: Atlas Books, W.W. Norton & Company, 2005.

Quinn, Susan. *Marie Curie: A Life*. New York: Simon & Schuster, 1995.

Redniss, Lauren. *Radioactive: Marie & Pierre Curie: A Tale of Love and Fallout*. New York: It Books, HarperCollins, 2010.

FOR YOUNG READERS

O'Quinn, Amy M. *Marie Curie for Kids*: *Her Life and Scientific Discoveries*. Chicago: Chicago Review Press, 2016.

Steele, Philip. *Marie Curie: The Woman Who Changed the Course of Science*. Washington, DC: National Geographic Children's Books, 2008.

For Meghan, Drew, and Arden —D.H.

For Danny —J.H.

Balzer + Bray is an imprint of HarperCollins Publishers.
Determined Dreamer: The Story of Marie Curie
Text copyright © 2024 by Deborah Hopkinson
Illustrations copyright © 2024 by Jen Hill
All rights reserved. Manufactured in Italy.

Library of Congress Control Number: 2023937085
ISBN 978-0-06-237332-8

The artist used gouache, watercolors, and digital tools to create the illustrations for this book.
23 24 25 26 27 RTLO 10 9 8 7 6 5 4 3 2 1

First Edition